The
Shakers

Edited and Introduced
by
Wim Coleman

The round stone barn at Hancock Shaker Village
Pittsfield, Massachusetts (Photo by Daniel Smith)

Discovery Enterprises, Ltd.
Carlisle, Massachusetts

© Discovery Enterprises, Ltd., Carlisle, MA 1997

ISBN 1-57960-005-0 paperback edition
Library of Congress Catalog Card Number 97-67539

10 9 8 7 6 5 4 3 2 1

Printed in the United States of America

Subject Reference Guide:

The Shakers
Edited and Introduced by Wim Coleman

The Shakers — U. S. History

The Shakers — Religion

The Shakers — Utopian Society in America

Photos/Illustrations:

Cover photo:
Eldress Minerva Reynolds and Ernest McLean,
son of Myra McLean, who died at Mt. Lebanon.
Published courtesy of the Fruitlands Museums, Harvard, MA.

Other illustrations and photos are credited where they appear in the text.

Table of Contents

Hands and Hearts:
The Lives and Ideas of the Shakers

by
Wim Coleman

They were called "Shakers" from the very beginning — and the name was not meant as a compliment. In their early days, they were notorious for explosive meetings during which they shook, jerked, trembled, convulsed, spoke in tongues, and generally behaved in a disruptive and undignified manner. Their sect was formally known as the United Society of Believers in Christ's Second Appearing, the Millennial Church, or the Alethians. But they shrewdly embraced the name "Shakers," thereby making it useless as an insult.

The Shakers were founded during the mid-eighteenth century in Manchester, England by James and Jane Wardley as a radical offshoot of the Quakers, otherwise known as the Society of Friends. But in 1758, a new member joined the sect and soon became its dominating force. This was Ann Lees, a blacksmith's daughter, later known as Mother Ann Lee. Ann was particularly devoted to the Shaker doctrine of celibacy, and came to believe that carnal relations between man and woman were the source of all the world's evils. Ann's zealotry got the Shakers into trouble on more than one occasion. She was infamous for disrupting Anglican services and destroying private property.

After serving a 1770 prison term for her activities, Ann was seen as more than merely the Shakers' leader; she was recognized as a new incarnation of Christ, returned to humankind in the body of a woman. Through a series of visions and revelations, Mother Ann became convinced that the future of her followers was in the New World. So in 1774, she took a tiny band of disciples to New England. From that time on, the Shakers were an American phenomenon; the Wardleys lost their influence as religious leaders and died in poverty.

After Mother Ann founded the first American Shaker community in Watervliet, New York, it took her several years to acquire American followers. But her potent message gradually took hold. She promised her disciples nothing less than redemption and paradise — not after death through heavenly grace, but during mortal life through works and deeds. Members began by renouncing carnal relations and confessing their sins. Once this was achieved, divine perfection became possible even for mortals.

It was only after Mother Ann's death in 1784 that the sect truly began to expand. This was in no small part due to the disciplined but benign leadership of her two most cherished American disciples, Father Joseph Meacham and Mother Lucy Wright. Father Joseph and Mother Lucy were loyal to Mother Ann's precepts of chastity and mortal salvation; they also emphasized the value of communal living. From their time on, the Shakers shared all their goods and property. Father Joseph and Mother Lucy also lent the sect an air of dignity it had never known under the flamboyant Mother Ann.

The Shakers expanded westward during the early nineteenth century. By the late 1820s, there were approximately twenty Shaker communities spread out between Maine in the east and Ohio, Kentucky, and Indiana in the west. These communities were very successful, profitable, and innovative. Today, the highly industrious Shakers are credited with important inventions in architecture, furniture design, and even technology. Their communities are also widely regarded as the most successful experiment in communal living ever attempted in the modern world.

The sect thrived and grew in an atmosphere of religious revivalism in early nineteenth-century America — and also a climate of experimentation in worldly utopias like George Ripley's community at Brook Farm in Massachusetts. After the Civil War (1861-65), these trends waned, and so did the Shakers. The sect then fell into a decline from which it has never recovered. But its influence upon American life remains.

This small book is not intended as a history of the Shakers. But perhaps it can give an impression of the rich diversity of Shaker life and thought — and also of the extraordinary contributions the Shakers have made to American culture.

Detail from Elder George Kendall's plan of the Shaker Village in Harvard, Mass., 1836. (Courtesy of the Fruitlands Museums)

Mother Ann Lee:
Prophetess and Foundress

The spirit of Mother Ann Lee, who instructed the Shakers to "put their hands to work and their hearts to God," hovers over the whole of Shaker life and history. Uneducated and illiterate, Mother Ann wrote nothing herself. But a Shaker "gospel" was written about her life and words, based on accounts of believers who knew her. This was the Testimonies of the Life, Character, Revelations and Doctrines of Mother Ann Lee. *The following passages have been excerpted from this book.*

Christ's Second Appearance

To the Shakers, Mother Ann was nothing less than Christ come again, offering a new chance for fallen humanity. The Testimonies *open with the following words, which describe the theological importance of Mother Ann's life to the Shakers. Here we get a suggestion of an important Shaker belief: that Christ and the deity are dual — both male and female. Hence, Christ's second appearance had to be in the form of a woman.*

Source: *Testimonies of the Life, Character, Revelations and Doctrines of Mother Ann Lee*, Albany, New York: Weed, Parsons & Co., 1833; reprinted, New York: AMS Press, Inc., 1975, pp. 1-2.

God, in His all wise providence, had laid the foundation of man's redemption in Judea, among the Jews, who were called his Chosen People. It was there the *First Born* in the *New Creation*, who was to be the Saviour of the world, was first revealed. There he fulfilled his ministry in his earthly tabernacle, and drank the full cup of his sufferings on earth; and from thence he ascended to His Father, that the way might be prepared for his Second Coming, in the female part of his manhood, for the travel of souls in the regeneration. And when the time was fully come, according to the appointment of God, Christ was again revealed, not in Judea, to the Jews, nor in the person of a male; but in England, to a Gentile nation, and in the person of a female.

This extraordinary female, whom, her followers believe God had chosen, and in whom Christ did visibly make his second appearance, was Ann Lee.

Ann Lee's Spiritual Crisis

Born in Manchester, England in 1736, Ann Lees (who later shortened her name to "Lee") was the daughter of a poor blacksmith. Perhaps against her own wishes and religious inclinations, she married another blacksmith named Abraham Standerlin. She bore him four children, all of whom died.

The deaths of her children brought Ann to a deep spiritual crisis. Already a member of a small religious sect led by James and Jane Wardley, Ann prayed intensely for understanding and peace. This is Ann's own account of an early revelation, retold by her American follower, Hannah Goodrich.

Source: *Testimonies…, op. cit.,* pp. 36-37.

"When I set out to obey the gospel, I cried to God to bring my sins to remembrance; and I confessed them one by one as I committed them; and I denied myself of every gratification of a carnal nature, of everything which my appetite craved, and ate and drank that which was mean and poor that my soul might hunger for nothing but God.

"I often rose from my bed in the night and walked the floor in my stocking feet, for fear of waking up the people. I did not let my husband know my troubles, lest I should stir up his affections, and I was careful not to lay any temptation before him. I also prayed to God that no man might suffer in hell on my account.

"Thus I labored in strong cries and groans to God day and night, till my flesh wasted away and I became like a skeleton, and a kind of down came upon my skin, until my soul broke forth to God; which I felt as sensibly as ever a woman did a child, when she was delivered of it. Then I felt unspeakable joy in God, and my flesh came upon me like the flesh of an infant."

Hope for a New World

Through visions and revelations, Ann soon came to believe that carnal relations between man and woman were the source of all evils in the world — including disease, poverty, hunger, and war. She became convinced that she herself could lead humankind out of sin and into redemption. The Wardleys and their followers believed her, and Ann rapidly took command of the sect, becoming known as "Mother Ann." The small band of believers, already called "Shakers," was persecuted, and Ann herself spent time in prison. There seemed no hope for the expansion of Ann's religious movement in England, so she and seven followers sailed to America in 1774.

During her first several years in New England, Ann failed to win any new converts. Then, in 1779, she found her most prized and important disciple. This was Joseph Meacham, who had participated in a failed Baptist revival. Searching for a new spiritual foundation, Meacham heard about Mother Ann and her little band of Shakers based in Niskeyuna, New York. Meacham sent a colleague to visit Mother Ann and question her about her doctrines. In reply, Mother Ann hinted at the Shaker belief in a dual deity.

Source: *Testimonies…, op. cit.*, pp. 16-17. (Unusual punctuation is preserved from the original source.)

…Joseph Meacham sent Calvin Harlow to Mother Ann with the following observation and query, namely: Saint Paul says, "Let your women keep silent in the Churches; for it is not permitted unto them to speak; but they are commanded to be under obedience, as also saith the law. And if they will learn anything let them ask their husbands, at home; for it is a shame to a woman to speak in the church. But you not only speak, but seem to be an Elder in your church. How do you reconcile this with the Apostle's doctrine"?

Mother Ann answered, "The order of man in the natural creation is a figure of the order of God, for man in the spiritual creation. As the order of nature requires a man and a woman to produce offspring, so, where they both stand in their proper order, the man is the first, and the woman the second, in the government of the family. He is the father, and she the mother, and all the children, both male and female, must be subject to their parents; and the woman, being second, must be subject to her husband, who is the first; but when the man is gone, the right of government belongs to the woman; so is the family of Christ."

This answer opened a vast field of contemplation to Joseph, and filled his mind with great light and understanding concerning the spiritual work of God. He clearly saw that the New Creation could not be perfect in its order, without a father, and a mother. That, as the natural creation was the offspring of a natural father and mother, so the spiritual creation must be the offspring of a spiritual father and mother.

He saw Jesus Christ to be the Father of the Spiritual Creation, who was now absent; and he saw Ann Lee to be the Mother of all who were now begotten in the regeneration; and she, being present in the body, the power and authority of Christ on earth, was committed to her; and to her appertained the right of leading and governing all her spiritual children.

A New Christ

After Meacham's conversion, the Shaker movement began to grow in America, although its followers suffered considerable persecution and even mob violence. Mother Ann was fully accepted by her disciples as a new Christ, capable of extraordinary miracles. Consequently, Shakers were not the least bit shocked when Mother Ann repeated the words of Jesus as if they were their own; compare the following passage with Matthew 11:27 in the King James Bible.

Source: *Testimonies…, op. cit.,* p. 232.

Mother Ann also spoke to a number of the Brethren and Sisters who were about taking their leave of her, to return to their homes, saying, "Go and tell your Brethren those things which ye see and hear; the blind receive their sight; the lame walk; the lepers are cleansed; the deaf hear; the dead are raised up; and the poor have the gospel preached to them; and blessed is he whosoever shall not be offended in me."

The Death of a Messiah

Mother Ann died in 1784 after an intensely-lived life of great accomplishments and great sufferings. Her words to her followers as she approached death added to her legendary stature.

Source: *Testimonies…, op. cit.,* pp. 259-260.

Ephraim Welch, being at Watervliet,[1] went into Mother's room to see her, at a time when she was under great sufferings, and asked her if he could do any thing for her comfort. She answered, "If you keep the way of God, it is all I desire, and the greatest comfort I can have in this world."

[1] Another name for Niskeyuna.

Mother Hannah Goodrich, being at Watervliet, a few days before Mother's decease, did not expect ever to see her out of her room again, but, one morning, as she was sweeping the piazza floor, Mother came out and said, "Sweep clean." "I will, Mother," replied Hannah. Again she said, "Ah, sweep clean I say." "I will," said Hannah. "But, I say, sweep clean," said Mother again. By this time Hannah perceived that Mother had reference to the floor of the heart, and said no more. Immediately Lucy Wright, subsequently called "Mother Lucy," who took care of her in her last sufferings, came and took hold of her hand, and asked her to go in. Mother answered, "I will. I will be obedient to you, Lucy, for I am married to you, and I will go with you." And they went in together.

As Mary Hocknell was watching with Mother Ann, a little before her decease, she said, "I see Brother William[2] coming in a golden chariot, to take me home." She then said to Mary, "Molly, poor child, I am about to go home, and after I am gone you will have many sorrows." Mother's words came to pass, for Mary passed through many scenes of sorrow and sufferings, after the decease of her dearest and best friend, who had brought her up from childhood.

[2.] Ann's brother, who died earlier the same year.

A Sense of Purpose

Until her death in 1784, Mother Ann led the Shakers through sheer force of personality. Partly due to her illiteracy, she never fully developed her own theology, so when she died, her followers suddenly found themselves wondering just what they believed and stood for.

Fortunately, Mother Ann was survived by her most valued convert, Joseph Meacham, who assumed leadership of the sect a couple of years after her death and promptly began to codify the doctrines, beliefs, and rules of the society. Meacham's synthesis of Mother Ann's ideas included two important themes:

1. *Equality of the Sexes.* Since Mother Ann had held that God was equally male and female, it was absurd for men to assume superiority over women. Soon after taking leadership of the sect as "Father Joseph," Meacham sought an eldress to share his office. He chose Lucy Wright, who had been near Mother Ann during her last days; she became "Mother Lucy," and her rank and powers were precisely equal to those of Father Joseph. From that time on, the entire Shaker leadership of ministers, elders, and deacons was divided equally between men and women.

2. *Communism.* Under Meacham's leadership, the Shakers came to hold all goods in common. They had gravitated toward this practice during Ann Lee's leadership, in no small part due to the deprivations and persecutions of an unsympathetic world. As Meacham saw it, their communism was perfectly in accord with the behavior of Christ's disciples as described in the New Testament: "And all that believed were together, and had all things common; And sold their possessions and goods, and parted them to all men, as every man had need (Acts 2:44-5)."

The spiritual and intellectual heirs to Father Joseph and Mother Lucy continued the work of shaping and defining Shaker beliefs and practices.

They produced many documents which made the goals and purposes of the Shakers ever more clear to an increasingly respectful world.

Principles and Regulations

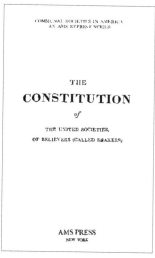

COMMUNAL SOCIETIES IN AMERICA
AN AMS REPRINT SERIES

THE

CONSTITUTION

of

THE UNITED SOCIETIES,
OF BELIEVERS (CALLED SHAKERS)

AMS PRESS
NEW YORK

*Title page from an 1833 edition
of the Shaker Constitution.*

Among these documents were various versions of the Shaker Constitution. An 1832 edition included a succinct and clear declaration of faith and principles.

Source: "A Brief Exposition of the Established Principles, and Regulations of the United Society of Believers called Shakers," Watervliet, Ohio: 1832. Contained in *The Constitution of The United Societies of Believers (Called Shakers)*, Watervliet, Ohio: 1833; reprinted, New York: AMS Press, Inc., 1978, pp. 4-5.

§I. Faith and Principles of the Society.

1. A life of *innocence and purity,* according to the example of Jesus Christ and his first true followers; implying entire abstinence from all sensual and carnal gratifications.

2. LOVE. — "By this shall all men know that ye are my disciples if ye have love one to another. Love is the fulfilling of the law." This is our bond of union.

3. PEACE. — "Follow peace with all men," is a divine precept; hence our abstinence from war and bloodshed, from all acts of violence towards our fellow men, from all the party contentions and politics of the world, and from all the pursuits of pride and worldly ambition. "My kingdom [said Christ] is not of this world."

4. JUSTICE. — "Render to every man his due. Owe no man any thing, but to love one another." We are to be just and honest in all our dealings with mankind, to discharge all just dues, duties, and equitable claims, as seasonably and effectually as possible.

5. HOLINESS. — "without which no man shall see the Lord." Which signifies to be *consecrated*, or set apart from a common to a sacred use. Hence arises all our doctrines and practical rules of dedicating our persons, services, and property to social and sacred uses, having adopted the example of the first gospel Church, in establishing & supporting one *consecrated & united* interest by the voluntary choice of every member, as a sacred privilege, and not by any undue constraint or persuasion.

6. GOODNESS. Do good to all men, as far as opportunity and ability may serve, by administering acts of charity and kindness, and promoting light and truth among mankind. "Whatsoever ye would that men should do to you, do ye even so to them."

7. TRUTH. This principle is opposed to falsehood, lying, deceit, and hypocrisy; and implies fidelity, reality, good earnest, sincerity, and punctuality in keeping vows and promises. These principles are the genuine basis of our institution, planted by its first founders, exhibited in all our public writings, justified by scripture and fair reason, and practically commended as a system of morality and religion, adapted to the best interest and happiness of man, both here and hereafter.

Who Could be a Shaker?

The Shaker Constitution was also very clear on the subject of how to qualify for membership in Shaker society.

Source: "A Brief Exposition...," *op. cit.,* pp. 6-7.

1. All persons who unite with us, in any degree, must do it freely and voluntarily, according to their own faith and unbiassed judgment.

2. In our testimony, both public and private, no flattery, nor any undue influence is used; but the most plain and explicit statements of our faith and principles are laid before the inquirer; so that the whole ground may be comprehended, as far as possible, by every candidate for admission.

3. No considerations of property are ever made use of, to induce any person to join us, nor to prevent any one from leaving us; because it is our faith, that no act of devotion or service that does not flow from the free and voluntary emotions of the heart, can be acceptable to God as an act of true religion.

4. No believing husband or wife is allowed, by our rules, to separate from an unbelieving partner, except by mutual agreement; unless the conduct of the unbeliever be such as to warrant a separation by the laws of the land. Nor can any husband or wife who has otherwise abandoned his or her partner, be received into communion with the Society.

5. Any person becoming a member must rectify all his wrongs, and, as fast and as far as it is in his power, discharge all just and legal claims, whether of creditors or filial heirs. Nor can any person, not conforming to this rule, long remain in union with the Society. But the Society is not responsible for the debts of any individual, except by agreement; because such responsibility would involve a principle ruinous to the institution.

6. No difference is to be made in the distribution of parental estate among the heirs, whether they belong to the society or not; but an equal partition must be made as far as may be practicable and consistent with reason and justice.

7. If an unbelieving wife separate from a believing husband, by agreement, the husband must give her a just and reasonable share of the property; and if they have children who have arrived to years of understanding sufficient to judge for themselves, and who chuse to go with their mother, they are not to be disinherited on that account. Tho the character of this institution has been much censured on this ground; yet we boldly assert that the rule above stated has never, to our knowledge, been violated by this Society.

8. Industry, temperance, and frugality are prominent features of this institution. No member who is able to labor, can be permitted to live idly upon the labors of others. All are required to be employed in some manual occupation, according to their several abilities, when not engaged in other necessary duties.

Leaving the Shakers

Because of their communism, the Shakers faced one especially serious dilemma. How were apostates to be treated when they left the order? Could they claim payment for work they had done for the community? Could they at least reclaim any belongings they had brought to the community upon their arrival? The Shaker Constitution argued to the contrary.

Source: "A Brief Exposition…," *op. cit.,* pp. 22-5.

[I]f the law grants the liberty of bestowing as a gift, it never can revoke the gift made under the sanction of that law; since all the blessings of a free government depend on the protection of life, liberty, and the enjoyment of property; the right of using property righteously acquired must, of course, be accounted one of its blessings.…

Here the Covenant is the evidence of the fact, that the with-drawing member did voluntarily give his property and services for the uses therein specified; and also that he therein promised never to make any charge or demand for the same.…

Most clearly, then, any one losing his right of membership, by renouncing his faith and his former obligations of obedience, has no better claims to privileges, property or support, than those who never were members. But those and those only who acknowledge and obey the faith and doctrines of the gospel, and conform to the rules and orders thereof, are held in relation as members.

Compensation for Apostates

Shakers seldom if ever actually carried out the strict terms of their rule denying apostates any right to compensation. When people joined the movement, a full account was taken of the belongings they brought in. When members departed, they received an equivalent repayment. They received no interest, nor any payment for work done for the society; but by far the majority of apostates left the society satisfied. The following document is a typical agreement signed by a departing Shaker.

Source: Edward Deming Andrews, *The People Called Shakers*, New York: Dover Publications, 1963, p. 67. (Transcribed from a 1789 manuscript in Andrews' library.)

Whereas I Pitman Cooke have heretofore professed myself to be of the Religious Society of Christians called Shakers and have frequently visited the Elders of the Church and have frequently Contributed for the Support of the Ministry and Table Expenses for myself and others that have Visited the Elders and for the Support of the poor of said Church and Society which I acknowledge I gave or Contributed freely and Voluntarily according to my own Faith and that it hath been Consumed in the Manner and for the purposes for Which I gave it. Notwithstanding since I have departed from them I have Conceived that I have Contributed more than my Just and equal proportion While I professed to be in union with them, And upon that consideration I have applyed to the present Elders of the Church to Consider me on that account And have Received of Elder David Meacham in behalf of the Church and Society the Sum or Value of Twenty one pounds two shillings New York currency as a Matter of Gratis on their parts Which together with what I have heretofore Received I do acknowledge myself fully Satisfyed with, and I do believe and acknowledge it to be

a Just and equal ballence. Therefore I do by these pre-
sents acquit and Discharge the said Church and Society
Jointly and Severally from any further Request, Charge
or Demand of any Kind or Nature Whatever....

A Successful Experiment

*The nineteenth century bred many utopian experiments in socialism
and communism. These included George Ripley's community at Brook
Farm in Massachusetts and Robert Owen's New Harmony Community in
Indiana. Most of these experiments were dismal failures. The Shakers
were a remarkable exception. They shared their belongings and the fruits
of their labor cheerfully, without any apparent resentment or envy. In fact,
the Shakers are today often credited with the most successful experiment in
communism in modern history. How did they accomplish this?*

*Elder Frederick W. Evans was one of the ablest Shaker thinkers of his
day. He came to the society while planning a utopian community based on
materialistic principles; the success of the Shakers taught him his mistake.
In this excerpt from his book* Shaker Communism, *Evans explains the
Shaker belief that communism must arise from a spiritual impulse, not a
material one.*

Source: F. W. Evans, *Shaker Communism; or, Tests of Divine Inspiration*, London: James
Burns, 1871; reprinted, New York: AMS Press, Inc., 1974, pp. 73-74.

By this "we know that we have passed from death unto
life, because we love the brethren."

The *absence* of true fraternal love amongst men has
produced the present evil condition of human society, in
all its relations, internal and external. By love, therefore,
the inhabitants of the new heavens and earth were to be
pre-eminently distinguished.

If a man really loves his neighbour as himself, it will

first as the outward and inferior be *visible* to "all men," by their equal participation between them of all earthly goods and substances; yet this is but the fruit and evidence of their equal participation in spiritual treasures pertaining to salvation.

If communion of earthly goods be sought as an *end*, it is of man; but if it follow as a consequence of an *inward principle* — love — it is of God.

A baptism of the Holy Christ — Spirit from the resurrection heaven effected it in a short time, within the first century of the Christian Era, by withdrawing man's affections from things below, and placing them on things above. They became transformed.

Jesus taught men to "take no thought" as to what they should eat, drink, or wear, as a *first* object, but to "seek *first* the kingdom of heaven and its righteousness," and promised that inferior necessary things "*should be added.*"

A strong desire for salvation *from sin* — the sin of selfishness — is the best preparation that a soul can have for community of interest in earthly things.

Sin and self produce *private* property.

Innocence and self-denial produce *community* of property.

The first Christian Church set before men an example of love — a oneness of interest in all things. And although the order was lost to the external view with the fall of the Church, yet men have never ceased to admire and try to imitate it, for the sake of temporal advantage — the *loaves and fishes.*

In all ages, and in a thousand ways and forms, the principle has been adopted and applied among men; but especially in our own day, and by our own generation.

Yet the object aimed at has invariably been diametrically opposite to that of *the men of Galilee* — loving souls baptised of Christ. They have sought *first* what they should eat and drink, and how they should be clothed.

The kingdom of heaven is where *love produces community*; but when man, from a selfish motive, seeks to build upon the foundation of "all things common," his building is a "man's building, and it is not able to stand."

Love to man is therefore a sure and certain criterion of all Divine Revelation. Anything contrary to, or short of, this test — love to man — emanating from the spirit-world of angelic life, is proof that it comes from an order of spirits that is *not* joined to the Church of Christ in that world, and who, therefore, are not proper ministers to "the heirs of salvation" who belong to the Church of Christ upon earth.

Engraving of Harvard Holy Hill of Zion, 1848. (From David Lamson's Two Years Experience Among the Shakers)

Shakers as Viewed by the World

In their quest for earthly perfection, the Shakers deliberately separated themselves from the rest of humanity, whom they referred to simply as "the world." This separation was far from complete. Shakers depended on the world for goods and necessities they couldn't produce themselves, and they sold products of their own industry. And of course, the celibate society depended upon the world for new recruits. The world's reactions to these strange visionaries varied tremendously — from intolerance and hatred to acceptance and even admiration.

The Trustees room at Harvard Shaker Village is furnished with typical Shaker furniture. 1950. The simple, functional designs were sought after by "the world," then and now. (Courtesy of the Fruitlands Museums)

Early Intolerance

During their early days in America, Shakers suffered considerable persecution and were even victims of mob violence. The period of the American Revolution (1775-83) was particularly trying. Shakers were strict pacifists and refused to fight for the Colonial cause, raising suspicions that they were actually in league with the British. This was a sad misconception; the Shakers were deeply sympathetic to the patriots, even if they were unwilling to take up arms on their behalf.

During this period, a Shaker apostate named Valentine Rathbun wrote several bitter diatribes against the Shakers, contributing greatly to a negative view of the sect. Rathbun even fabricated a bizarre "document" which supposedly proved Shaker collaboration with King George. In this passage from one of his pamphlets, Rathbun described the indoctrination of new members in nightmarish terms.

Source: Valentine Rathbun, *A Brief Account of a Religious Scheme*, Worcester, Massachusetts: 1782, pp. 11-12. (From the Western Reserve Historical Society Shaker Collection. Archaic typography has been modernized in this transcription.)

There is a very extraordinary and uncommon power attends their instructions; in the first place, a total blindness, as to all their former views of religion and the Bible, on the instructed, takes place; and then a strange infatuation of the mind, to believe all their teachers say. Presently a strange power begins to come on, and takes place in the body, or human frame, which sets the person to gaping and stretching; and soon sets him to twitching, as though his nerves were all in a convulsion. I can compare it to nothing nearer in its feelings, than the operations of an electrifying machine; the person believes it is the power of God, and therefore dares not resist, but wholly gives way to it. — Thus the power comes on, more and more; and as the power increases, so their faith increases in their teachers. If any body opposes them, it brings on the power quick, strong and violent; and they cry out, on the opposer, that he will be damn'd, for opposing the power of God; and fall to twitching and trembling, as though they had an extreme fit of the ague.

Col. Smith's Attack

Hostility toward the Shakers increased as their communities expanded westward during the early years of the nineteenth century. They were accused of deliberately destroying families and even of witchcraft. In a widely-read 1810 pamphlet, Col. James Smith made many accusations against the Shakers — most of them false and some of them bizarre. In this passage, Smith accused the Shaker leadership of corruption and exploitation.

Source: Col. James Smith, *Remarkable Occurrences Lately Discovered Among the People Called Shakers, Of a Treasonous and Barbarous Nature; or, Shakerism Developed,* Carthage, Tennessee: William Moore, 1810, p. 13. (From the Western Reserve Historical Society Shaker Collection.)

The Shakers are a hidden people, they say they are not of this world, and all others they call the *world*, and have no connection with them, only to buy or sell whatever they can, so as to make gain or to bring money to their treasury. Their leaders, I believe, live in ease and luxury, and conceal their principle views from the lower class, who are slaves. One of the men…who had left them told me, he believed that Elder David [Darrow] stored up liquor for their own use, which was as far as possible concealed from the common people. He said that he saw Elder David's steward at one time buy several barrels of rum and wine, which were taken to his lodging.

Smith went on to accuse the Shakers of beating laborers and children, and even of castrating their males. In this passage, he described the future influence of the Shakers in apocalyptic terms.

Source: Smith, *op. cit.,* pp. 14-15.

Let Shakerism predominate, and it will extirpate Christianity, destroy marriage and also our present free government, and finally depopulate America. According to their scheme civil and ecclesiastical governments are blended together, theirs is a despotic monarchy.

Bemused Tolerance - Nathaniel Hawthorne

Shaker communities thrived tremendously in the years after Smith's diatribe — without causing the destruction of Christianity, marriage, or American freedom. Consequently, overt persecution waned. Even so, people found it difficult to understand the values of the sect.

For example, author Nathaniel Hawthorne (1804-1864) visited the Shakers and wrote two stories about them: "The Canterbury Pilgrims" and "The Shaker Bridal." The latter, especially, displays more than a few negative ideas about Shakers. Hawthorne assumed that the believers were rigid, fanatical, and emotionally impoverished.

The following passage is from "The Shaker Bridal." In this tale, a man and woman — formerly in love but now celibate — are being tested by a group of elders to become the leaders of a Shaker community. Note at least two misconceptions in this short paragraph. Men who joined the Society were not permitted to abandon unbelieving wives and children to "the mercy of the world." More importantly, Hawthorne's panel of elders consists only of men — an impossibility in the sexually egalitarian world of the Shakers.

Source: Norman Holmes Pearson, ed. *The Complete Novels and Selected Tales of Nathaniel Hawthorne*, New York: Modern Library, 1937, p. 1013.

They [the elders] had overcome their natural sympathy with human frailties and affections. One, when he joined the Society, had brought with him his wife and children, but never, from that hour, had spoken a fond word to the former, or taken his best-loved child upon his knee. Another, whose family refused to follow him, had been enabled — such was his gift of holy fortitude — to leave them to the mercy of the world. The youngest of the elders, a man of about fifty, had been bred from infancy in a Shaker village, and was said never to have clasped a woman's hand in his own, and to have no conception of a closer tie than the cold fraternal one of the sect. Old Father Ephraim was the most awful character of all. In his youth he had been a dissolute libertine, but was converted by Mother Ann herself, and had partaken of the wild fanaticism of the early Shakers. Tradition whispered, at the firesides of the village, that Mother Ann had been compelled to sear his heart of flesh with a red-hot iron before it could be purified from earthly passions.

A Poetic Query

Like Nathaniel Hawthorne, the American actress Charlotte Cushman (1816-1876) visited the Shakers and saw only cold joylessness in their lifestyle. Cushman wondered how Shakers could leave behind youthful ambitions, shirk the glories and duties of war, or abandon the joys of married life. Did they have no warm blood in their veins? She expressed her skepticism in the following verses.

Source: *The Shaker*, Vol. I, No. 1, January 1871, Albany, NY: Mt. Lebanon Bishopric, p. 7. (From the Western Reserve Historical Society Shaker Collection. Several verses have been edited out, for lack of space. The occasionally eccentric punctuation in the following two entries is preserved from the original source.)

Lines, Suggested by a Visit to the Shakers, near Albany.
by Charlotte Cushman

1.   Mysterious worshippers! ·
    Are ye indeed the things ye seem to be.
    Of earth, yet of its iron influence free
       From all that stirs
    Our being's pulse, and gives to fleeting life
    What well the Hun termed "the rapture of the strife?"

2.   Are the gay visions gone,
   Those day dreams of the mind by fate there flung,
   And the fair hopes to which the soul once clung?
        And battled on;
   Have ye outlived them? All that must have sprung
   And quickened into life when ye were young?...

4.   Has not ambition's paean
   Some power within your hearts to wake anew
   To deeds of higher emprise — worthier you,
        Ye monkish men,
   Than may be reap'd from fields? — do ye not rue
   The drone-like course of life ye now pursue?...

6.   Have ye forgot your youth
   When expectations soared on pinions high,
   And hope shown out in boyhood's cloudless sky,
        Seeming all truth —
   When all look'd fair to fancy's ardent eye,
   And pleasure wore an air of sorcery?…

8.   Ye would have graced right well
   The bridal scene, — the banquet or the bowers,
   Where mirth and revelry usurp the hours —
        Where, like a spell,
   Beauty is sovereign, where man owns its powers
   And woman's tread is o'er a path of flowers.

9.   Yet seem ye not as those
   Within whose bosoms memory's vigils keep,
   Beneath your drooping lids no passions sleep,
        And your pale brows
   Bare not the tracery of emotions deep —
   Ye seem too cold and passionless to weep!

A Verse Reply

A Shaker sister, who signed her work only with the initials "S.E.," replied to Cushman's poem with some biting verses of her own. S.E. took particular issue with Cushman's Victorian vision of men rightfully reigning over women. These tart closing stanzas of S.E.'s poem refute the then widespread notion that the Shakers were bereft of wit and irony.

Source: *The Shaker, op. cit.,* pp. 7-8.

"Man owns its powers?" — and what will man *not* own
To gain his end, to captivate, dethrone?
The truth is this, whatever he may feign.
You'll find your greatest loss his greatest gain;
For like the bee he will improve the hour,
And all day long he'll buzz from flow'r to flow'r,
And when he sips the sweetness all away,
For aught he cares the flowers may all decay.

But here each other's virtues we partake,
Where men and women all those ills forsake;
True virtue spreads her bright Angelic wing,
While saints and seraphs praise the Almighty King.
And when the matter's rightly understood,
You'll find we labor for each other's good;
And this, Charlotte Cushman, is our aim,
"Can you forego this strife, nor own your shame?"

Now if you would receive a modest hint,
You'd keep your *name* at least, from public print,
Nor have it hoisted, handled round and round,
And echoed o'er the earth from mound to mound,
As the great advocate of (O, the name!)
Now can you think of this, nor "own your shame?"
But Charlotte, learn to take a deeper view
Of what your neighbors say, or neighbors do;
And when some flattering knaves around you tread,
Just think of what a SHAKER GIRL has said. S.E.

Praise from Parker

*Eventually, some of the best minds in America began to admire the Shakers'
experiment with utopian socialism, even if they still had reservations about
Shaker theology. In this letter of 1848, the abolitionist clergyman Theodore
Parker (1810-1860) spoke highly of the sect's goals, achievements, and doctrines — with one important exception.*

Source: John Weiss, *The Life and Correspondence of Theodore Parker,* New York: Appleton,
1864, Vol. I, p. 384.

What you said in your last note about the superiority
of the domestic economy of the Shakers, I am not only
ready but happy to admit. Certainly, you have no menial
service — none of your community think work is degrad-
ing; while, in society at large, many men are ashamed of
work, and, of course, ashamed of men (and women) who
work, and make them ashamed of themselves. Now, the
Shakers have completely done away with that evil, as it
seems to me; that is one of their great merits, and it is a
very great one. At the same time, they secure comfort,
and even wealth; the only charge that I can bring against
them is that of the neglect of marriage. In an argument
you would very likely say a great many things against
marriage, and all connection between the sexes; but still,
the fact remains that God created men and women, and
left the perpetuation of the race to the union of the two,
doubtless intending that marriage — of one man with
one woman — should continue so long as the race should
endure.

It seems to me, also, that some of the best qualities of
human nature are developed by the connection. I look
on it as much a spiritual as a carnal want. It seems to me
that the omission of this is the great defect of the Shakers.

31

Praise from Emerson

Other remarkable thinkers were less reserved in their praise. The transcendentalist philosopher Ralph Waldo Emerson (1803-1882) first visited a Shaker community in the company of Nathaniel Hawthorne. Unlike Hawthorne, Emerson considered the Shaker experiment to be astoundingly successful. He greatly admired their mixture of communism and capitalism and was deeply impressed by their ethical behavior, as he expressed in this paragraph from his essay "Worship."

Source: Ralph Waldo Emerson, *The Prose Works of Ralph Waldo Emerson*, Boston: Riverside, 1879, Vol. II, p. 441.

In the Shakers, so called, I find one piece of belief, in the doctrine which they faithfully hold, that encourages them to open their doors to every wayfaring man who proposes to come among them; for, they say, the Spirit will presently manifest to the man himself, and to the society, what manner of person he is, and whether he belongs among them. They do not receive him, they do not reject him. And not in vain have they worn their clay coat, and drudged in their fields, and shuffled in their bruin dance, from year to year, if they have truly learned thus much wisdom.

Howells on Shaker Humor

William Dean Howells (1837-1920), one of the most influential American writers of his time, had the following to say about the Shakers in Shirley, Massachusetts.

Source: William Dean Howells, *Three Villages*, Boston: 1884, p. 108. (Found in Edward Deming Andrews, *The People Called Shakers*, New York: Dover Publications, 1963, pp. 327-328.)

I should be sorry to give the notion of a gloomy asceticism in the Shaker life. I saw nothing of this, though I saw

self-restraint, discipline, quiet, and heard sober, considered, conscientious speech. They had their jesting, also;
and those brothers and sisters who were of a humorous
mind seemed all the better liked for their gift of laughing
and making laugh.

Correspondence with Tolstoi

*By the end of the nineteenth century, the Shakers had achieved world-
wide fame and respect. As far away as Russia, their achievements had
caught the attention of the celebrated novelist and essayist Count Leo Tolstoi
(1828-1910). Tolstoi was delighted to receive letters and tracts from the
Shaker Elder Frederick W. Evans. In this reply, Tolstoi queried Evans about
the secrets of the Shakers' success.*

Source: Leo Tolstoi and F. W. Evans, *Shaker-Russian Correspondence, Between Count Leo
Tolstoi and Elder F. W. Evans,* Mt. Lebanon, NY: 1891. (From the Western Reserve Historical
Society Shaker Collection.)

Toula, Tasnaya Poliana, Russia,
February 15, 1891.

ELDER FREDERICK W. EVANS.

Dear Friend and Brother: Thank you for your kind letter.

It gave me great joy to know that you approve of my
ideas upon Christianity. I was very much satisfied with
your views upon the different expression of religious
sentiments, suiting the age of those to whom they are directed.
I received the tracts that you sent me, and read them, not
only with interest, but with profit; and cannot criticise
them, because I agree with everything that is said in them:
there is only one question which I should wish to ask you.

You are (as I know), non-resistants. How do you manage to keep communal property-but nevertheless, prop-

erty? Do you acknowledge the possibility, for a Christian, to defend property from usurpators? I ask this question because I think that the principle of non-resistance is the chief trait of true Christianity; and that the greatest difficulty, in our time, is to be true to it: how do you manage to do so in your community?...

With sincere respect and love,

Yours truly,

(Signed)   LEO TOLSTOI.

Evans' Reply

The articulate and learned Evans responded with a brilliant letter clarifying Shaker pacifism. Note in the following passages the irony of earlier allegations against the Shakers: that they believed in the welding of the church and state and opposed basic American liberties. In this letter, Evans made clear that the Shakers had always held quite the opposite view.

Source: Tolstoi and Evans, *op. cit.*, pp. 2-3.

MT. LEBANON, N.Y., U.S.A.
March 6, 1891.

LEO TOLSTOI.

Dear Friend and Brother: Your welcome letter of the 3d ult. was duly received....

All the great European nations are Christian: and war is a permanent institution among them. They are exhausting their national resources, either in fighting, or "in peace, preparing for war." Do they not all pray to the same God, to help them to kill each other? Could the devil do any worse by them?

Evans went on to explain the Shaker belief that Jesus himself was not without sin, since surely he confessed sins to John upon his Baptism. Moreover, Jesus was not God himself but an "elder brother" of humankind who learned exceptionally well from his own disobedience to the "Christ spirit." As Evans put it, "He was simply 'the first-born of many brethren' just as Ann Lee was the first born of many sisters." To propose otherwise was to suggest that Jesus could not grow and learn, which was to deny a basic Shaker tenet, that of human perfectibility.

Source: Tolstoi and Evans, *op. cit.*, pp. 5-7.

Not until the separation of church and state, by "the horns" (infidel powers) "that grew out of the beast," in the American Revolution — could communal property be held by non-resistants. That is the "New Earth"; and as the new earth becomes more perfect in its righteousness, the "New Heavens" will be nearer to perfection, in all Christian virtues....

We, the Shakers, hold and defend our communal property under the civil laws of "the new earth:" but in no case, or under any circumstances, should we injure a fellow being. You see that our civil government is the voice of the people, *"vox populi, vox Dei"*;[3] and the people, who are the rulers, are more progressed than are the rulers of Russia, or of any church and State government on the face of the earth. Consequently, we (the Shakers) can, under the American secular government, carry out the abstract principles taught by the Christ-spirit's revelation, more perfectly than has, hitherto, ever been done by mortal men and women....

F. W. EVANS.
Mt. Lebanon, Columbia, Co., N. Y.

---

[3] "The voice of the people is the voice of God."

Shaker Voices

The Shakers were not generally given to vain and worldly activities like journal-keeping. Consequently, while Shaker literature is rich in songs, stories, and theological writings, a smaller record survives of the personal, everyday joys and rigors of Shaker life. But the brothers and sisters who did leave behind memories of their lives were very eloquent, indeed. And the experiences they described were varied and fascinating.

Two Shaker Conversions

Ever since the first Shaker communities were founded, outsiders have tended to think of believers as passive, non-individualistic followers. This view is far from accurate. During the height of Shaker culture in the nineteenth century, all sorts of people from all classes and walks of life were drawn to Shaker communities — some wealthy, some poor; some learned, some illiterate. And despite its emphasis on conformity, Shaker life allowed for considerable individuality of belief and expression.

The two first-person narratives which follow illustrate this fact. They both describe conversions to Shakerism, but the converts could hardly have been more different. One was a well-educated English thinker with a materialistic bent. The other was an African-American woman with little education. Even after becoming Shakers, both maintained highly individual voices and viewpoints.

Frederick W. Evans

Frederick W. Evans (1808-1893), whom we met in Chapters 2 and 3, seemed as unlikely a convert to Shakerism as can be imagined. A deist, materialist, and radical socialist during his early adulthood, Evans did not expect to find his utopian dreams realized in a religious setting. But in 1830, he paid a visit to the Shakers in Mount Lebanon, New York, and his life was permanently changed. At the time of his visit, he was participating in a plan to found a completely non-Christian socialist community. When he arrived in Mount Lebanon, he was traveling in search of "a suitable location in which to start."

Source: F. W. Evans, *Autobiography of a Shaker, and Revelation of the Apocalypse,* New York: American News Co., 1888; reprinted, New York: AMS Press, Inc., 1973, pp. 16-21.

Calling one day in the month of June (3rd), 1830, at the office in Mount Lebanon, I was directed to the North House as the proper place for inquirers. I was kindly received by those who, at that time, I supposed were the most ignorant and fanatical people in existence. And knowing by experience how touchy and sensitive *religious* persons were to any ideas not in unison with their own, and how extremely reluctant they were to have either their dogmas or practices tested by logic or common sense, I was very wary and careful as to what I said, and in the questions I propounded. But I was agreeably surprised and impressed by the air of candor and openness, the quiet self-repose, with which I was met. I remained here two or three days, but failed to find the touchy place where anathemas supply the place of reasoning, proof, and evidence; I have now been here some thirty-eight years, and have yet to find it. In fact, after about a week's inquiry, I pronounced them a society of infidels; which indeed was paying them the highest compliment of which I was capable....

The Shakers prayed for me, and I was met in my own path just as the Apostle Paul was met in *his* own path, by spiritual manifestations made to myself when quite alone, from time to time, during several weeks, until my reason was as entirely convinced, by the evidence received, of the existence of a spirit-world, as I am, by evidence that is presented to my outward senses, of the existence of our material earth. Not only so; but I came to a conception of the inner world as being the most substantial, and of the inner man as being the real man; the outward world being only the shadow of the invisible world of causation. I also saw a meaning in the words of Paul: "We look not at the things which are seen, but at the things that are not seen; for the things which are seen are temporal, but the things that are not seen are eternal."…

One night, soon after retiring, I heard a rustling sound, as of the wind of a flock of doves flying through the window (which was closed) towards my bed; and, that I believed it to be supernatural, and that the faith in the supernatural, which the servants had planted in my soul, by their oft-told *ghost* stories, had not wholly died out under my Materialism, was evidenced by the fact that I was frightened, and hid my head beneath the bed-clothes.…

I soon recovered my self-possession, and found that a singular mental phenomenon was going on. I was positively *illuminated*. My reasoning powers were enhanced a hundred-fold. I could see a chain of problems, or propositions, as in a book, all spread out before me at once, starting from a fact that I *did* admit and believe; and leading me, step by step, mathematically, to a given conclusion, which I had *not* hitherto believed. I then discovered that I had powers within me that I knew not of. I was multiplied and magnified, and intensely interested. I was *reasoning* as I never before reasoned.…

These visitations recurred nightly for three weeks, always different, always kind and pleasant; but were addressed directly to my rationality, showing me the facts of the existence of a spiritual world, of the immortality of the human soul, and of the possibility and reality of intercommunication between souls and spirits out of the mortal body....

At the end of three weeks, I was one day thinking of the wonderful condescension of my spirit friends, and how I had been met, to repletion, by evidence addressed to all my senses, powers, and faculties of body and mind: and I said to myself, "It is enough."...

Among the people (Believers) themselves, I had, for the *first time*, found religionists who were also rationalists, ready to "render a reason for the faith and hope that was in them;" and who were willing to have that *reason* tested by the strictest rules of logical ratiocination. And they could appeal to me, as a Materialist, as did the Nazarene to unbelievers, "If ye believe not my words" (and the validity of my arguments), yet "believe for the very works' sake."

Rebecca Jackson

Rebecca Jackson (1795-1871) was a free African-American born in Philadelphia. She spent her childhood in poverty and was prone to visions and revelations from a very early age. She left her husband to become an itinerant preacher and had loyal followers even before joining the Shakers. Eventually, she became an eldress and founded a Shaker community in Philadelphia consisting largely of African-Americans. Mother Jackson learned to read and write as a middle-aged woman, specifically so she could relate her religious journey. Here are some excerpts from Jackson's description of her conversion to Shakerism.

Source: Jean McMahon Humez, ed., *Gifts of Power: The Writings of Rebecca Jackson, Black Visionary, Shaker Eldress*, Massachusetts: The University of Massachusetts Press, 1981, p. 162. (Humez's brackets indicate likely interpolations by Alonzo G. Hollister, an early editor of Jackson's writings.)

December, 1842, my first visit with the people called Shakers, in company with Nathaniel, and Allen [Pierce],

Mary S. Lloyd, Polly [Ostrander]. We were kindly received. They asked me many questions, which I answered, and they asked if we would stay all night. I told them I would be pleased to stay if they would let us, though we could not stay now, but we would come again. One of the Sisters put her hand on my head and said, "Don't you wish you had a Mother?" I looked at her and smiled, and she gave me a book. Nathaniel Fry, Allen Pierce, Mary S. Lloyd, Polly Ostrander was all standing by, but did not see it. But I did not know it.

We bid them farewell and returned home. I then said to them, "Don't you see they are the true people of God?"...

Jackson and her companions paid another visit to the Shakers about a year later. This time, Jackson's destiny as a Shaker was fully revealed to her.

Source: Humez, *op. cit.*, p. 164.

The next day, the 17th January, 1843, I went again to see Believers, with Nathaniel and Allen Pierce, Mary S. Lloyd. They received us kindly. Nathaniel Fry and Allen Pierce went back, Mary S. Lloyd and I stayed. The same evening they took us over to see some of the Sisters, where they sung us some heavenly songs [of Zion]. And I was asked many questions which I answered in the fear of God and in prayer. For this was the teaching which I received from the beginning, and I have always obeyed this counsel to this day. When anybody speaks to me, on any occasion, I always pray for knowledge to be able to answer them right, and in truth, that I may please God in all I say and do. So we visited, till it was time to return and retire to rest.

*That night, Jackson received a vision of a female spirit she had first en-
countered in 1834. She was also visited by "shining, holy, and heavenly
messengers of peace and salvation." The following day, the Shakers continued praying for her.*

Source: Humez, *op. cit.*, p. 165-166.

They spoke to me about confessing my sins. This I
did not understand. I saw in them much concern about
my confession, and I desired to give them all the satisfac-
tion that in my power lay. And as I done nothing without a gift of God, I now made this a subject of solemn
prayer to Almighty God, to teach me what he would have
me to do. And while I was sitting in solemn silent prayer,
one of the Sisters came in who speaks for angels and holy
spirits. And while she stood, I was told to get up and
walk the floor, which I did. And I felt such a flowing of
the spirit of peace! She walked to the door as if she was
going out. Afterward she turned herself around to me
and began to speak in the new tongue, which was in the
spirit. "'Oh, thou blessed woman,' thus saith the holy
angel, 'I have had charge of thee lo these many years,'"
with many more words in the same tongue, bowing herself and waving her hands in obedience to the holy angel,
who she was then aspeaking for. Then she began to speak
in the unknown tongue, and the spirit of God like a tide
overwhelmed me, and I saw the angel that I saw a year
ago in a dream — which was made known to me at that
time that it had charge of me.[4] This strengthened my
faith....

...when I went to tea, the first mouthful I took, I was
told, "Don't eat one mouthful till you confess." I took

---

[4] Jackson first encountered this angel in 1842.

the mouthful out of my mouth and tied it in the corner of my pocket-handkerchief. And the Lord was to make the way. I felt to wait His time and will. So I went to bed. In the morning I went to the table. I did not eat. I was now praying for the way to be made, and watching closely that I might see the way when it was made....

Between breakfast and dinner, they brought a sleigh and took us to the South House [for this was the door to the Church.] ...When we got to the place, they received us with the same kindness as they did at the Church. I saw in the mind of them the same concern about my confession, which I was waiting for, when the way was made, according to the light which I had received.

The Shakers continued their interrogation, sometimes to the frustration of Jackson, who felt that she was not being allowed to confess and testify in a way which felt natural to her. After thirty hours of fasting, the Shakers allowed Jackson to eat. Finally, she received a vision of Mother Ann Lee herself.

Source: Humez, *op. cit.,* p. 168.

At night we went to meeting and while they were worshipping God, I saw the head and wings of their blessed Mother in the center of the ceiling over their heads. She appeared in glorious color. Her face was round like a full moon, with the glory of the sun reflecting from her head, formed itself into a round circle with glorious lights reflecting from it in streams which formed a glorious crown. And her face in the midst. And she was beautiful to look upon. Her wings was gold. She being in the center, she extended her golden wings across the room over the children, with her face toward me and said, "These are all mine," though she spoke not a word.[5] And what a Mother's look she gave me. And at that look, my soul was filled with love and a motion was in my body, like one moving in the waves of the sea. I was happy. And I felt to embrace all her children in the arms of my soul. I understood by one of the discerners that there was sixteen angels in the room that night. I only saw our Blessed Mother, and that was as much as I was able to bear. We went to our room. Mary knowed nothing about the holy visitors.

William Byrd

Frederick Evans and Rebecca Jackson both served the Shakers successfully (if sometimes contentiously) for many years. Some Shaker lives were shorter and sadder. Such was the case of William S. Byrd (1806-1829), who was descended from a prosperous and influential family. William's father, Charles Byrd, was an Ohio judge concerned with violence against Shakers. Charles became deeply sympathetic with Shaker beliefs and considered joining the sect. Although he himself did not, he was pleased when his son did.

William wrote these letters to his father while in his early twenties; in fact, he only lived to be twenty-three. In them, William described a community in a state of doubt and transition.

Source: Stephen J. Stein, ed., *Letters From a Young Shaker: William S. Byrd at Pleasant Hill*, Lexington, Kentucky: University Press of Kentucky, 1985, pp. 84-86.

Pleasant Hill, March the 9th, 1828

Dear Father,

...As I wrote you my health is better than it was when you were here, and I enjoy more tranquility of mind than

---

[5] This vision, it seems, was experienced as a silent picture, with the inner voice adding interpretive words. [Humez's note.]

43

I did then, but at the same time I feel it my duty as you are my parent, and one that has expressed a desire to know my situation from time to time, to tell you that although I can write and talk some about happiness, I am far from the enjoyment of that state of felicity which is in reserve for the righteous. On the contrary the life I lead is a life of great, and daily suffering, and this suffering is not a little increased by the view I have of futurity, nevertheless I must confess that I am thankfull for this light that I have been favoured with, and believe from my heart that it is necessary, and that it has been sent to me by an all wise God to enable me the better to bear the cross which he has laid upon me, for although I can sensibly feel the love of God in my soul, and consequently enjoy some happiness, yet it is mixed up with so much mental and bodily affliction, especially the former, that I could not it appears to me keep soul and body together, if it was not for the prospect I have of attaining to that happiness without the least mixture of alloy which God has promised to those who by a patient continuance in welldoing will finally overcome all things....

Your Son,
William S Byrd

Source: Stein, *op. cit.*, pp. 93-95.

Pleasant Hill, 19th of June, 1828

Dear Father,

...The Society continues to decrease in number, though I hope not in quality, for on the contrary I do confidently

believe that there is an increase in the body, of righteousness and peace, but to mention the names of those who
do from time to time apostatise would be tedious to me,
and perhaps uninteresting to yourself, as you know but
few of them. I therefore have generally omitted to record
in my letters the names of those that leave us, I will now
however mention two members a man and his wife with
whom you were acquainted, and you will I have no doubt
be surprised to receive the intelligence if you have not
heard it already, as they were both at the time you were
with us for any thing you knew to the contrary, prominent Believers — namely Elder James Guest, and Lucy his
wife. Lucy continued here some months after her husband
went away, during which time he visited her occasionally,
and she poor creature whom you once considered allmost
a saint on earth, like her Mother Eve, listened to the arguments of the enemy of souls until she was finally overcome.
As I mentioned above I expect you will be surprised to hear
of the fall of Lucy and her husband, but at the same time
if you were as well acquainted with them, and their history
as I am, you would not be in the least affected by it....

I must now I believe conclude and remain Your Son,

With true regard,
William S Byrd

Mother Ann's Work

The malaise William Byrd described in Pleasant Hill was a problem in other Shaker communities of the time. The society seemed to have reached a height of growth and prosperity, and many of its members didn't know where to turn next. Disunion and apostasy set in. By 1837, the Shakers badly needed a spiritual revival — and they got one.

In that year, young girls began to have visions and revelations. Soon, mystical experiences became more and more widespread among adult believers. The ensuing period, known in Shaker lore as "Mother Ann's Work," lasted little more than a decade, but was enough to renew Shaker faith and spirituality.

The following passage describes the funeral of Abijah Worster in 1839. Worster was the last surviving founder of the Harvard community, and his funeral became a truly extraordinary event — attended not merely by Shaker mortals, but by the spirits of departed Shakers, Mother Ann, Jesus Christ, and the male-female deity worshipped by the society.

Source: *Extract from an Unpublished Manuscript on Shaker History*, Boston: 1850), pp. 12-13. (Found in Edward Deming Andrews, *The People Called Shakers*, New York: Dover Publications, 1963, pp. 156-157.)

[A]n inspired Shaker girl stood at the door, to take down the names of those old friends from the spirit world, who were expected to attend the body to the grave, in honor of Father Abijah. This girl said there were all the first Shakers present. Father Abijah was very much gratified in seeing his old friends. The old man adjusted the head in the coffin, and asked Mother Ann if she thought he had changed much, she answered no, Abijah, it looks well. (These questions are always asked and answered by the Visionist.)

We are told that Father Abijah marched out at the head of the coffin, singing a beautiful freedom song. The Pall

Bearers were the Eternal Father, the Eternal Mother, Christ and Mother Ann. The brethren marched out of the house from one door, the sisters from another, preceded by the Elders, falling back a distance from the body to give room to the heavenly guests. The spirits lingered around the grave till their brethren of earth had left the yard, — then Power and Wisdome, Christ and Mother struck up a lively dance, when all the spirits joined hands and danced right merrily around the grave. — At the close of the dance the Godhead *crossed hands forming a seat* for Father Abijah, — and giving a glad shout spread their wings and ascended, followed by the heavenly host to Mother's mansion, where a banquet was in waiting to welcome the last of the first Fathers in Harvard to his final home.

A Link to the Past

The decline of the Shakers is generally said to have set in around the time of the Civil War. Nevertheless, Shaker communities survived for well over a century afterwards, as did the Shaker way of life. Sister R. Mildred Barker (1897-1990) lived more than eighty-five years among the Shakers in Maine and left behind a rich collection of writings and recollections. Her words form a remarkable bridge between our own time and the Shaker past. Sister Mildred was adopted by the Shakers as a little girl. Here is the beginning of her story, told in her own words.

Source: William Randle, *The Shaker Heritage*, Cleveland: Western Reserve University, 1960-1961, Side 12. (Transcription of Randle's recording found in Gerard C. Wertkin, *The Four Seasons of Shaker Life*, photographs by Ann Chwatsky; New York: Simon & Schuster, 1986, pp. 121-122.)

I went to the Shakers on July 7, 1903, a very hot July day. I remember leaving Providence [Rhode Island] on the train early in the morning. It seemed to me I rode all day long and…I guess we must have ridden most of the day because I didn't get to Alfred until about five o'clock at night, when I was met there by one of the brethren with a horse and buggy — such was the transportation we used in those days! — and I was taken to the Trustees' Office (my mother also was with me) and we stayed there overnight. And in the morning Eldress Fannie Casey who was the Eldress at Alfred at the time…and by the way she also had been the one who was instrumental in taking me there, came down to the Office to see us and with her she brought Eldress Harriett Coolbroth from the Second Family at Alfred and…I had…become a little bit attached to Eldress Fannie, probably because she was going to send me down to the Second Family with Eldress Harriett…and, however, I was told to go so I went down to the Second Family. At that time there was just one little girl about my own age there and I was…I didn't seem to be very happy to start with and I remember sitting out back of the house on a swing, planning that when they weren't watching me so well and they got a little used to me and I didn't know everything that I did, that I'd run down across the pasture and up over the mountain and go home to Providence. However, by the time they didn't watch me so well, I had changed my mind and I never did try that trip across the mountain! I grew very, very fond of Eldress Harriett. She was the mother that I needed and as a young child I thought that there couldn't possibly be anyone any lovelier.

*Elder Greaves, with tools in hand, was featured on
a postcard from Mt. Lebanon, New York.*

Shaker Twilight

As the official diarist of the Sabbathday Lake community, Sister Mildred recorded these poignant New Year meditations late in her life.

Source: Sister R. Mildred Barker, "Home Notes from Sabbathday Lake, Main," *The Shaker Quarterly 7*, Sabbathday Lake, Maine: United Society of Shakers, Spring 1967, p. 10. (Found in Wertkin, *op. cit.*, p. 63.)

The New Year crept in unceremoniously upon us. No bells or fanfare heralded its entrance for most of us had long ago learned that those who "watch the year out" never see it leave. Like the Shaker child who, seeing New Hampshire for the first time, said, "Why, I don't see that it looks any different from Maine," one sees no difference between the old and the new years that are but an instant apart. Yet we know that there is a difference, for one closes the door on the triumphs and defeats, the hopes and disappointments, and the joys and sorrows of the past twelve months, and the new year holds in its tiny hands opportunity, a forward look, a fresh beginning and new courage. So we go forward knowing that He who holds the universe in His hand and guides the planets in their course is not unmindful of His children and will supply "strength according to our needs."

Shaker Industry

Try to imagine today's world without washing machines, metal-pointed pens, flat brooms, or common clothespins. These are just a few of the inventions credited to the Shakers. They are also believed to have invented the screw propellor and the steam turbine. Perhaps the most visible contribution of the Shakers to today's world comes by way of their architecture and furniture. Shaker designers and woodworkers were instructed to forego beauty and adhere to the sacred principles of "use" and "order." The effect was paradoxical, for Shaker architects and carpenters produced works of spare, fresh beauty. Today, we are surrounded by furniture, homes, and buildings influenced by the Shakers.

A great objection to communistic societies is that they destroy the work ethic and human initiative. So how did the communistic Shakers give the world so many new, beautiful, life-enhancing things? In Chapter 2, we heard Elder Frederick W. Evans' explanation. Unlike most communistic societies, the Shaker outlook was spiritual and nonmaterialistic. Work was a form of worship, a way of praising God, not mere drudgery. The inven-

Some typical items designed and crafted by the Shakers

tion of a device which bettered material life always brought a fallen world just a step backward toward paradise — or forward toward heaven. How better to praise God, Jesus, or Mother Ann?

Moreover, the Shakers showed a particular genius in their business dealings. With the world at large, they were capable capitalists, selling products of their communal labor at advantageous prices. They found it easy to compete with the world; their furniture, fabric, metalwork, and other goods were almost invariably superior to anybody else's. And of course, Shaker profits equally benefited everybody in the community; no one was exploited by anyone else.

Varied Work

The Shakers realized that work had to be tolerable and even joyful if it were to serve as form of prayer. Overwork was detrimental to this spirit, as was monotony. Although work was a large part of the everyday routine of all Shakers, overwork was actively discouraged. Shakers were also encouraged to take up as many different skills as possible so that their labors would remain stimulating and engaging.

Modern day interpreter at Hancock Shaker Village in Pittsfield, MA (by Daniel Smith)

Here is an excerpt from the journal of a teenage Shaker named Benjamin Gates, who became an elder as an adult.

Source: Edward Deming Andrews, *The People Called Shakers*, New York: Dover Publications, 1963, pp. 109-110. (Transcribed by Andrews from a Shaker manuscript.)

September 1832

S	1st	Helped clean out the ditches in the swamp so as to let the water on the meadow.
M	3d-	Ploughing and harrowing above the south orchard with the old horses chief part of the time, and the rest of the time drawing dung from Jones's on the flat.
W	5th	The family move in to the house! …But me no go, that to my sorrow…
M	10th	I help finish sow the wheat
T	11th	Draw dung
W	12th	Help clean up the taylors shop, and geather [gather] myself in
Th	13th	Help cut onion seed; began a blue jacket for Hiram Rude
Fr	14th	AM. go down to the grist mill and mend conductors PM cut onion seed
S	15th	Work on Hiram's jacket
M	17th	I work on Hiram's jacket
Tu	18th	I finish jacket, & do various choars
W	19th	I began a blue jacket for Philip B.
Th	20th	I help shingle the hog pen
S	22nd	I finish Philip's jacket, & do various choars
M	24th	Began a blue jacket for Benjamin Lyon
Tu	25th	I finish said jacket
W	26th	I go butternutting with Rufus Hinkley
Th	27th	Began a jacket for Aaron Bill, thick blue
Fr	28th	I work at the north house, preparing hoof and horn for buttons

Sisters' Work

Shaker men inclined toward work like heavy farming, blacksmithing, and carpentering, while women gravitated toward more domestic duties like sewing, housekeeping, and cooking. But between these two poles, the work of men and women overlapped considerably. For example, Sister Tabitha Babbitt is credited with inventing a Shaker version of the circular buzz saw. And in addition to more traditional duties, Sister Elizabeth Lovegrove tailored, painted windows, and burned brush in an orchard. She also served as a nurse. The following is an excerpt from her journal of the 1830s. It offers a glimpse of the medical practices of the nineteenth-century Shakers.

Source: Andrews, *People Called Shakers, op. cit.*, p. 159. (Transcribed by Andrews from a Shaker manuscript.)

Betsey B. takes Phisic

Elder Sister is relieved some of her cough by the vaper bath and electricity.

Lucy Bishop here to help sweat Elder Ebenezer with hemlock and hot stones.

Commence polticeing Amy's face with camomile and Marsh mallows.

Elder sister fell down and hurt her side-we resort to shocking rubbing and bleeding her, likewise apply skunk cabbage leaves and make her tea of Johnswort and pepper grass seed, all have a good effect.

Rachel Sampson severely afflicted with the sun headache, apply a blister to the neck and arm also oint the forehead with marrow of hogs jaw and apply a bag of hops wet with vinagar, good effect.

Collaboration with the World

As relations between the Shakers and the world grew friendlier during the nineteenth century, believers and non-believers discovered that they had much to offer each other.

The following passage, written for a Shaker advertisement, tells the story of Dr. Louis Turner, a non-Shaker authority on herbal medicines. Due to a general shortage of acceptable herbs, Dr. Turner turned to the Shakers of Union Village, Ohio for a better supply. It turned out to be a very fruitful and profitable collaboration. (Incidentally, the life span of the average Shaker actually was markedly longer than that of other Americans.)

Source: *The Influence of the Shaker Doctor*, Cleveland: Union Village Society, 1850. (Western Reserve Historical Society Shaker Collection. Found in Amy Bess Miller, *Shaker Herbs: A History and a Compendium*, New York: Clarkson N. Potter, 1976, pp. 100-101.)

...Dr. Turner...was met at Lebanon the nearest R.R. station by the oldest member of the society, and on the way was impressed by this venerable man that here was evidence, of not only a knowledge of the laws of health, but a keen insight into scientific, and experienced medication, and how life may be prolonged in its full vigor. Dr. Turner was first shown through the Botanical Garden which had been established for so many years, and which he saw was in the best possible condition. Such plants as are improved by the care of man were here seen to almost give out their medical qualities without any manipulation, while those which flourish best under the retiring influence of shade and moisture remained undisturbed.

Men and women were busy collecting portions of the plants, which had reached the proper state, under the direction of the Shaker Doctor J. R. Singerland, who was introduced to Dr. Turner, and informed of the object of his visit.

Postcard, advertising headache remedy

They together paid a visit to the Laboratory, where the plants were being carried and where they were to be made into powerful and palatable medicines....Nothing could be more complete than the arrangement of vats, receivers, etc., which he saw in the interior of the medical laboratory.

The Shaker Doctor before referred to [Singerland], asked to examine the formulas for his medicines which

Dr. Turner had brought with him, and he was not long in discovering that the advice and influence of the Shaker Doctor would be worth considering. A discussion arose as to some worthy changes, and after a full and free exchange of ideas, which had the combined experience and learning of these two men, resulted in producing a line of medicines; which have accomplished wonderful results for good, and which is alike gratifying to patient and doctor.

Seeds for Sale

Perhaps in no enterprise did the Shakers excel as much as in the manufacture and sale of garden seeds. The Shakers revolutionized this industry and were probably the first to package seeds in paper bags. They also sold seeds in attractive wooden display boxes to retailers.

Mt. Lebanon seed catalog

Shaker Expressions

The Shakers regarded their artistic, musical, and literary expressions as extensions of their industry. The standards of "order" and "use" applied in all areas of Shaker life; a poem, a painting, a dance, or a hymn was expected to be as useful as a chair, a barn, or a meeting-house. Moreover, most Shaker art remained anonymous; the work and its use were ultimately more important than the artist.

Song and Dance

The Shakers of the nineteenth century were especially famous for their ceremonial singing and dancing. In an 1857 feature article in Harper's, *writer Benson John Lossing related the events of a typical ceremony. He began by describing the arrival at the meeting house of some six hundred non-Shaker spectators (who themselves were separated according to sex), then the arrangement of the male and female Shakers on opposite sides of the broad meeting-house floor. These excerpts pick up with the beginning of the ceremony.*

Source: Don Gifford, ed., *An Early View of the Shakers: Benson John Lossing and the* Harper's *Article of July 1857*, Hanover, New Hampshire: University Press of New England, 1989, pp. 35-39.

The worshipers soon arose, and approached from opposite ends of the room, until the two front rows were within two yards of each other, the women modestly casting their eyes to the floor. The benches were then instantly removed. There they stood in silence, in serried columns like platoons in military, while two rows of men and women stood along the wall, facing the audience. From these came a grave personage, and standing in the centre of the worshipers, addressed them with a few words of exhortation. All stood in silence for a few minutes at the conclusion of his remarks, when they began to sing a hymn of several verses to a lively tune, and keeping time with their feet. In this, as in all of their songs and hymns, they did not pause at the end of each verse, but kept on without rest and with many repetitions until the whole hymn was completed....

After two other brethren had given brief "testimonies," the worshipers all turned their backs to the audience, except those of the two wall rows, and commenced a backward and forward march, or dance, in a regular springing step, keeping time to the music of their voices, while their hands hung closely to their sides. The wall rows alone kept time with their hands moving up and down, the palms turned upward. The singing appeared like a simple refrain and a chorus of too-ral-loo, too-ral-loo, while all the movements with hand, foot, and limb were extremely graceful.

The worshipers now stood in silence a few moments, when they commenced singing another hymn, with chorus like the last. When it was ended they retired to each end of the room, the benches were replaced, and the men and women again sat down opposite each other. Elder [Frederick W.] Evans then came forward, and, in an able discourse of almost an hour, expounded the peculiar doctrines of the Shakers....When he had ceased all the worshipers arose, the benches were removed, and they formed themselves into serried ranks as before. Then, with graceful motions, they gradually changed their positions into circular form, all the while moving with springing step, in unison with a lively tune. In the center stood twenty-four singers in a circle, twelve men and twelve women; and around them, in two concentric circles, marched and countermarched the remainder of the worshipers, the men three and the women two abreast. A brief pause and they commenced another lively tune and march, all keeping time with their hands moving up and down, and occasionally clapping them three or four times in concert. The women were now three and the men two abreast. When the hymn ceased, with a prolonged strain, they all turned their faces toward the inner circle of singers.

A nineteenth-century print of a Shaker dance. Note the elegantly-dressed woman on the lower left and the man's top hat on the lower right. Outsiders attended many Shaker ceremonies, much as they attended concerts or the theater.

After another pause the worshipers commenced a hymn in slow and plaintive strain. The music was unlike any thing I had ever heard; beautiful, impressive, and deeply solemn. As it died away, the clear musical voice of a female was heard from the external circle, telling, in joyful cadence, how happy she felt as a member of that pure and holy community. To this many among the worshipers gave words of hearty concurrence. Another sweet female voice then commenced a hymn in which "Mother Ann" was celebrated. The entire body of worshipers formed into a single line, marched slowly around the central circle of singers, and as the strain ceased their hands fell gracefully to their sides, their bodies were inclined gently forward, and their thin hands were slowly raised and clasped over the waist.

After a brief pause they commenced singing a lively spiritual song. The worshipers now formed four circles, with the singers as the central one, and held each other by the hand, the men and women separately. These circles symbolized the four great Dispensations — the first from Adam to Abraham; the second from Abraham to Jesus; the third from Jesus to "Mother Ann"; and the fourth the present, which they hold to be the millennial period. In this hymn they sang of UNION. as exhibited by their linked hands; and when it had ceased they all lifted up their hands, and gave a subdued shout — the shout of victory — the final victory of Christ in all the earth, and the triumphs of the Shaker, or Millennial Church.

Three or four more songs and hymns, with graceful dances or marches, and the ceremonials drew to a close. While singing the last sweet song, the men and women took their respective places at each end of the room, and stood facing each other. Elder Evans then addressed a few words of encouragement to them, and stepping forward, thanked the audience for their kind attention, and informed them that the meeting was closed.

A Shaker Hymn

The following "Hymn of Love," a fairly early composition, is typical of songs sung at such a ceremony.

Source: Thomas Brown, *An Account of the People Called Shakers*, Troy, New York: Parker and Bliss, 1812; reprinted, New York: AMS Press, Inc., 1972, pp. 371-372.

Loving Brethren, loving Sisters,
    Middle ag'd and blooming youth,
Lay aside your Sirs and Misters.
    Love the plain and simple truth.
Love's the spring of our communion,
    Life and breath of the new man;
Never was such love and union,
    Never since the world began....

Let us then not be mistaken,
    As to what we're call'd to love;
Whether things that may be shaken,
    Things below or things above.
First divide the flesh and spirit,
    Good from evil separate;
Then the thing that's void of merit,
    We must love not, we must hate.

Love not self that must be hated,
    Love not Satan, love not sin;
And to the flesh though you're related,
    Love not flesh nor fleshly kin.
Love not riches, honour, pleasures,
    Love no earthly, vain delight;
But the gospel, hidden treasure,
    You may love with all your might....

Singing in Tongues

In the days of Mother Ann Lee, a Shaker ceremony was hardly the orderly affair witnessed by nineteenth-century spectators like Benson John Lossing. Shakers did considerably more than merely shake. They jerked, twitched, convulsed, spoke in tongues, and even barked like dogs in an exercise known as "treeing the devil." After Joseph Meacham assumed leadership of the society in the 1880s, Shaker ceremonies became more organized and ritualized.

This is not to say that the spirit of wildness vanished from Shaker worship for good. The revival period of the 1830s and 40s known as "Mother Ann's Work" reintroduced some of the more outrageous antics of Shaker worship. Here, for example, is a song in tongues, credited to Hannah Ann Agnew of New Lebanon.

Source: Edward Deming Andrews, *The Gift to be Simple: Songs, Dances and Rituals of the American Shakers*, New York: J. J. Augustin, 1940, p. 78.

Hoo haw hum necatry O necatry O
Hoo haw hum necatry O cum
Ne holium ne-holium ne-catry O ne-catry O
Ne holium ne-holium ne hoo haw hum.

O werekin werekin catry catry
Werekin werekin catry coo
O werekin werekin catry catry
Werekin werekin catry coo.

Spiritual Foolery and Drunkenness

Another element of wildness in Shaker worship was the exercise of "throwing fool." One worshipper would declare him- or herself to be a fool and proceed to behave an imbecilic manner. Then the worshipper would "throw fool" to someone else, who would behave the same way. This was an exercise in both spiritual humility and pure hilarity.

In a similar spirit were songs of spiritual drunkenness and intoxication. These were sung while dancing, staggering, and reeling in a crazed, drunken manner. The following song of unknown origin is an example.

Source: Edward Deming Andrews, *The Gift to be Simple: Songs, Dances and Rituals of the American Shakers*, New York: J. J. Augustin, 1940, p. 63.

Drink ye of Mother's wine,
Drink drink drink ye freely,
Drink ye of Mother's wine
It will make you limber.

If it makes you reel around,
If it makes you fall down
If it lays you on the floor
Rise and take a little more.

The whirling gift

Epilogue

by
Wim Coleman

What could be more peaceful than this scene at
Hancock Shaker Village? (Photo by Daniel Smith)

People sometimes describe the Shakers as "extinct." This is hardly correct. At the date of this writing (1997), seven practicing members are still living in the village of Sabbathday Lake in Maine. As long as a single Shaker lives, one cannot wholly discount the possibility of a Shaker revival-particularly in a world as full of doubt and uncertainty as ours is today.

Even so, there is hardly any question that the society is in a decline — and it has been a very long decline, indeed. Because the Shakers were so astoundingly successful in almost every other respect, this decline is generally blamed on the sect's insistence upon celibacy. Celibacy seemed to guarantee that the society would eventually collapse due to lack of growth. True, the Shakers did adopt many children. And they educated them in schools of such high quality that many of the world's children attended them, too. But once these children became adults, they were not bound to the Shakers in any way and often left. Ultimately, the only hope for the Shakers of on-going growth was continuous religious revival, and this hope evaporated after the Civil War.

Nevertheless, it is a bit paradoxical to blame Shaker decline on the sect's celibacy, which clearly also played an important role in its success. Celibacy drove believers' thoughts away from family relationships and toward the community as a whole — a helpful outlook in their case. Celibacy was therefore not, as nineteenth-century critics of the Shakers often suggested, merely a weird quirk in an otherwise sensible philosophy. Regardless, it did help ensure the Shakers' decline.

Whatever their eventual fate, the Shakers continue to haunt us. Their doctrines are especially fascinating. They believed that the earth — fallen since the says of Adam and Eve — could be redeemed through human labor, and that we mortals could climb closer and closer to heaven until we reached it. They believed that the mortal, worldly life of the flesh and the immortal, unworldly life of the spirit could be made one and the same — if just a few of the world's wanderers "put their hands to work and their hearts to God."

Such experiments are always important, whether they fail or succeed. In the words of Oscar Wilde, a contemporary of the Shakers and also a socialist, "A map of the world that does not include Utopia is not worth even glancing at, for it leaves out the one country at which Humanity is always landing. And when Humanity lands there, it looks out, and, seeing a better country, sets sail. Progress is the realisation of Utopias."

The Shakers would surely agree.

Suggested Further Reading

In addition to sources of the cited excerpts, the following materials are recommended for further research:

Adams, Charles C., Ph.D. *The New York State Museum's Historical Survey and Collection of the New York Shakers*. Albany: University of the State of New York, 1941.

Andrews, Edward Deming and Faith Andrews. *Shaker Furniture: The Craftsmanship of an American Communal Sect*. Photographs by William F. Winter. New York: Dover 1950.

_____. *Work and Worship: The Economic Order of the Shakers*. Greenwich, Connecticut: New York Graphic Society.

Catalogue of Garden Seeds Cultivated by the Shakers at South Union, KY. Bowling Green, Kentucky: Gazette Print, 1884; from the Western Reserve Historical Society Shaker Collection.

Stein, Stephen J. *The Shaker Experience in America*. New Haven: Yale University Press, 1992.

Wiggin, Kate Douglas. *Susanna and Sue.* Cambridge, Massachusetts: 1909.

Wisbey, Herbert A. Jr., *The Sodus Shaker Community.* Lyons, New York: Wayne County Historical Society, 1982.

About the Editor

Wim Coleman is a freelance writer who lives in Chapel Hill, North Carolina. With his wife Pat Perrin, he has collaborated on two novels and a non-fiction book, as well as numerous works for educational publishers. *Terminal Games*, their suspense thriller about computer networking, was published by Bantam Books in 1994; foreign language editions have appeared in Japan, Germany, Italy, and Brazil. An award-winning playwright, Coleman became fascinated by the Shakers a year ago, while researching an opera libretto based on Nathaniel Hawthorne's *The Shaker Bridal*.

Both Wim and Pat have edited and introduced several other titles for this *Perspectives on History Series*.